Original title:
Tropical Dawn

Copyright © 2025 Creative Arts Management OÜ
All rights reserved.

Author: Isaac Ravenscroft
ISBN HARDBACK: 978-1-80581-660-7
ISBN PAPERBACK: 978-1-80581-187-9
ISBN EBOOK: 978-1-80581-660-7

Secrets of the Dawn

Sunrise sneaks in with a grin,
Blowing the night's sleepy din.
A rooster crows, or is it a crow?
The secrets above are ready to show.

Palm trees wiggle, shake their hair,
Sandy critters dance without a care.
Coconut shells become our hats,
When laughter rolls in with morning chats.

Awakening the Island Heart

The sun yawns wide, then spills its cheer,
As island dreams draw near and near.
A crab challenges a flip-flop fight,
While seagulls giggle at the sight.

A smoothie bar plays morning tunes,
And hula dancers sway with prunes.
Banana peels slip, oh what a sight!
The island heart beats with pure delight.

Morning Bliss on Velvet Beaches

The ocean whispers sweet and low,
As beach balls bounce to and fro.
With sunscreen battles waged in jest,
Laughter surrounds like a warm nest.

Flip-flops tango, and towels collide,
As beachgoers join the wacky ride.
Waves come in with a splish and splash,
Bringing mischief, fun, and a dash.

Reflections of a Waking World

Mirrors of water shimmer and shake,
As turtles play hide and seek with a flake.
Sunbeams tickle the palm tree leaves,
While giggles scatter like summer sheaves.

Coconuts roll like bowling balls,
And sandcastles rise, then inevitably fall.
With a splash and a whoop, the day begins,
As we dance in suits and silly fins.

Paradise Unfurls at Dawn

The sun yawns loud, a bright oops!
A drowsy rooster spills the beans.
Monkeys swing with morning scoops,
While palm trees dance in playful scenes.

Coconuts drop like silly bombs,
As waves crash with a giggle fight.
A parrot screeches, singing psalms,
In this uproar of sheer delight.

Garden of Light

Flowers stretch like yawning cats,
Cheerful blooms in rainbow rows.
A lizard wears a sunhat,
As buzzing bees compose their prose.

The gardener slips on fresh muck,
Clumsy boots in a muddy spree.
He grins wide, can't help but chuck,
Nature's slapstick comedy.

A Canvas of Awakening

Bright colors splatter across the sky,
Brushstrokes of laughter greet the morn.
An artist spills coffee with a sigh,
Smeared pastels of playful, worn.

He trips on a canvas, paints his toes,
As seagulls cackle overhead.
With stained hands, he strikes a pose,
A masterpiece made of humor instead!

Glimmering Waters

Waves roll in like giggling kids,
Splashing fish with silly flair.
A crab can't hide its silly lids,
Dancing sideways like it's light as air.

The sun winks at the glistening tides,
While swimmers squeal in playful fright.
With all the fun that nature provides,
Every splash feels just right at night.

Awakening Shores

The seagulls squawk, they lead the show,
As flip-flops slam, the beach-goers flow.
Sandcastles rise with a wobbly throne,
While crabs join in with a little moan.

Coffee spills as waves tickle toes,
Funny hats dance in the morning's glow.
Surfboards waiting, giggles in line,
It's a circus of joy, oh isn't it fine!

Whispering Palms

Palm trees gossip about last night's fun,
They chuckle softly as the day has begun.
A coconut drops, it's a fruity surprise,
Watch out below! It's a danger in disguise.

Sandy toes wiggle, umbrellas pirouette,
Laughing kids chase what they can't quite get.
A beach ball flies, hitting someone's drink,
Splashing all around—oh, what do you think?

First Light Over Emerald Waters

Emerald waves dance a silly jig,
As dolphins jump like they're in a gig.
The surfboard's lost, gone astray again,
Two folks chase it—letting out a hen!

Frothy bubbles tickle beneath the sun,
With jellyfish wearing a jellybean bun.
Mornings here, filled with laughter and cheer,
Fishy faces grin—'Good day, my dear!'

Sunrise Serenade

The sun peeks up like a sleepy cat,
While coffee brews, smelling quite phat.
Birds in hats sing their morning tune,
"Don't forget to dance, or you'll miss the moon!"

Beach towels spread, but one takes flight,
Soaring high like it's ready for a fight.
A flip-flop lands on a very bold crab,
And that little guy is ready to nab!

Luminous Horizons

The sun creeps up with a giant grin,
Rubbing its eyes, it stretches, let the fun begin.
Parrots in pajamas start a morning spree,
Who knew sunrise could be so silly and free?

A coconut drops, it hits a snoozing cat,
Who leaps like a dancer in a bright yellow hat.
The waves laugh as they tickle the sand,
While fish flip and flop; isn't nature so grand?

The Promise of a New Day

Roosters crow like alarm clocks gone wild,
While the sloths take their time, oh-so-styled.
Breezes blow mischief, a playful embrace,
As a crab moonwalks, it's a comical race.

Sunlight spills like juice from a clumsy cup,
Dancing between palm trees, lifting spirits up.
Lizards chuckle at the morning's bright charms,
In this wacky paradise, nothing does harm.

Emerald Leaves in Morning Haze

Emerald leaves giggle under dew,
As ants march in line, quite confused, it's true.
A chameleon sneezes, changing its hue,
While frogs croak their songs, like a band overdue.

A monkey swings by, wearing a funny hat,
He takes a pose, oh, imagine that!
Flowers burst out laughing, all colors unveiled,
In this jungle of joy, no laughter is jailed.

Golden Kisses on the Sea

The sea sparkles gold, tickling toes with glee,
A fish pops up, saying, "Come swim with me!"
Surfers tumble like pancakes, oh what a sight,
While seagulls play catch with the morning light.

A beach ball bounces, and oops, it flies high,
Landing on a boat; what a lucky guy!
The tide claps its hands, cheering in delight,
As the day begins with merry, pure light.

Dawn's Ethereal Lace

The sun peeks out, a playful tease,
Dancing shadows on the trees.
Coffee brews, a fragrant laugh,
Birds chirp tales on morning's half.

A cat sprawls wide, a regal pose,
Dreams of fish from sleepy prose.
Golden rays, a sticky grace,
Waving at the day's embrace.

The Rapture of Rising Sun

The roosters crow in funny tones,
While clumsy goats dance on their own.
Flip-flops flop on sandy shores,
As laughter echoes, the day restores.

A lazy wave from Mr. Crab,
As sunbeams tickle, a gentle jab.
No rush at all, just giggles loud,
As morning wraps us in a shroud.

Colors of Calm

Pink and orange paint the sky,
As sleepy eyes begin to pry.
Silly clouds in hats of fluff,
They float around, like kids in scruff.

Coconut trees with goofy bends,
Wave hello to all their friends.
Whispers of warmth, a gentle call,
As daydreams tease us one and all.

A New Day's Dance

With every step, the waves giggle,
Their foamy dance, a ticklish wiggle.
Footprints left in sandy lines,
Like treasure maps for hidden finds.

The sun winks bright, a cheeky grin,
As flip-flops fly, and kids dive in.
Every moment, a playful chance,
In nature's lively, sunny dance.

Velvet Skies

The world wakes up, a sleepy giggle,
Colors splash, a dance, a wiggle,
Birds in a chorus, cawing in tune,
While the sun yawns, bright as a cartoon.

Palm trees sway, doing the twist,
Nature's beauty, you can't resist,
Coconuts fall, a comical thud,
Creating laughter, like a playful flood.

Playful monkeys swing with glee,
Chasing shadows, feeling so free,
A roving lizard joins the parade,
Contorting in silliness, unafraid.

The gentle breeze tickles the day,
Spreading joy in a cheeky way,
Oh, the magic of morning's cheer,
As velvet skies make all things clear.

Ocean's Awakening Whisper

The waves chuckle, a frothy laugh,
Telling secrets from their shiny path,
A crab sidesteps, with a stylish flair,
Shells giggle softly, floating in air.

Seagulls squawk, like an off-key band,
While dolphins prance, a splashy stand,
Fish flip-flop in a comical race,
As the sun finds its joyous place.

Seaweed sways, a shimmery wig,
As the tides dance, they laugh and dig,
A treasure chest claps, so full of dreams,
Bursting with bubbles, flowing like streams.

Morning's laughter curls through the foam,
Where all the silly sea creatures roam,
With every ripple, a chuckle so sweet,
Ocean's whisper, where joy is complete.

The Bloom of New Hope

Flowers giggle, their petals spread wide,
As the sun tickles them, no need to hide,
Bumblebees buzz with a comical grace,
They dance from bloom to bloom, all in place.

Grass is soft, with a shortcut grin,
While ladybugs waltz, a spin to begin,
A butterfly sneezes, releasing a cheer,
As the garden awakens, blessings draw near.

Worms pop up, with a cheeky cheer,
Sharing their stories, loud and clear,
Through laughter they wiggle, so bold, so spry,
While blooms paint the ground beneath the sky.

Ah, the joy of the blossoms all around,
Silly moments, a happiness found,
In the warmth of the light, life's simple scope,
We embrace every giggle, a bloom of hope.

Sunrise Weaving

Sunlight stretches, a lazy yawn,
Weaving shadows, as day is born,
A cat falls from a fence with a thud,
Landing in a puddle, splashing with mud.

Children dance, in pajamas all bright,
Chasing after critters, a morning delight,
Sandy toes and giggles that soar,
As laughter ripples on the sandy shore.

The kite tangles in a clumsy twist,
Fighting the wind, a hilarious fist,
Chasing it down, feet bound to race,
As smiles stretch wide, we embrace the chase.

With a sunrise painting the world anew,
Each ray whispers laughter, all around too,
In this quilted morning, life's funny schemes,
We weave our dreams with giggles and beams.

Soft Shadows of First Light

When roosters boast and strut, quite bold,
The sleepy sun, a new day unfolds.
Lizards dance in pajamas, a sight,
As trees yawn, stretching in morning light.

Coconuts roll like balls on the sand,
While monkeys launch from branches, so grand.
A flip-flop lost, it's a game of chase,
With crabs as referees, full of grace.

The beach chairs wave hello with cheer,
While surfboards gossip, saying, "Get near!"
Palm leaves rustle, secrets afloat,
As seagulls plot mischief, that's the note.

In this goofy world, laughter does bloom,
With sunbeams bouncing, chasing away gloom.
Breezes carry tickles, a fun morning treat,
In the glow of first light, all hearts skip a beat.

The Golden Case of Morning

Golden rays peek through leafy seams,
Fluffy clouds pretend, weaving dreams.
Caffeine crabs dance on their tiny feet,
While fish play tag, calling it a feat.

Parrots sing gossip, feathers a-flare,
Waking sleepy sloths, caught unaware.
Alligators sunbathe, wearing shades,
As island jokes float in sun-baked parades.

A turtle in shades makes quite a scene,
As he shuffles to join the morning routine.
Bubbles of laughter rise up from the sea,
In this wacky world, feeling so free.

Golden sun ticks on the ocean's face,
While jellyfish twirl, oh, what a race!
With every tick of the clock, the vibe grows,
In the early light's warmth, anything goes.

Swaying Dreams in Light

The palm trees sway, doing their jig,
As the sun grins wide, feeling quite big.
Bikini-clad dolphins leap high with glee,
The world's a stage, oh what a spree!

Funky iguanas wear hats with flair,
While beach balls bounce high, not a care.
Seashell trumpets call to the shore,
As flip-flops skip, begging for more.

Sunburned tourists chase after a kite,
With sunscreen slathered, it's quite a sight.
Shells whisper gossip, tales of the tide,
In this silly kingdom, we take pride.

The warm winds giggle, tickling our toes,
As laughter echoes where the sea flows.
In this place where joy gets the light,
Swaying dreams arise, making hearts take flight.

Early Rays of Paradise

Morning whispers on the ocean's breath,
Fish are laughing at their breakfast death.
With grasshoppers jogging on sandy tracks,
And coconuts cheerleading, waving flags.

A crab in a hat struts with great style,
With sandy little shoes, he walks a mile.
Sloths on scooters race down the lane,
In this paradise, who needs the mundane?

Hammocks sway like gossiping friends,
While the sun juggles warmth that never ends.
Laughter spills as the day wears a crown,
Everything's fun when the sun's up and down.

With early rays spinning tales in delight,
Every creature, from shy to the bright,
Together they bask, a whimsical sight,
As the day breaks forth in a glorious light.

Secrets of the Sunrise

Morning stretches, yawns awake,
The rooster crows, a grand mistake.
Coffee spills upon the floor,
It's a circus, nothing more.

Sunglasses on, we hit the beach,
With sunscreen lessons yet to teach.
Flip-flops fly and seagulls swoop,
We laugh as we join the loop.

A Symphony in Coral

Fish in tutus, dancing free,
Coral reefs host quite the spree.
Crabs in tuxedos on parade,
Laughter echoes, never fade.

The seaweed wiggles, shakes a leg,
Starfish join the song, no beg.
Bubbles pop, and giggles swell,
Underwater, all's quite well!

Prism of Early Light

A parrot steals my morning toast,
As I, the sleepy breakfast host.
Sunbeams bounce like kids at play,
While juice spills bright like a bouquet.

Pancakes stacked, they seem to float,
A syrup river on my coat.
We laugh as we chase the dog,
Around the yard, through thick fog.

Hues of Hope on Water

Boats are bobbing, hats go flying,
A fish jumps high, while we're just sighing.
Splashing water makes us squeal,
In this madness, joy's a deal.

Sunset turns mischievous too,
With colors bold, a funny hue.
The ocean giggles, crabs all dance,
In this watery, wild romance.

The Calm Before the Paradise Storm

The roosters sing their early tune,
While the coconuts are dreaming soon.
A crab does a disco on the sand,
Waves giggle like they have a plan.

The sun peeks out, it winks and sways,
Seagulls plan their loudest praise.
Fish flaunt their scales, what a sight,
In this quirky morning light.

A Brush of Sun on the Ocean's Face

The sun paints stripes in shades of gold,
While shrimp in shades of scandal unfold.
A surfboard catches a flash of fun,
Pandemonium for everyone!

The waves laugh loud, they tickle toes,
A beach ball bursts, that's how it goes.
Laughter echoes from the shore,
As flip-flops chase the ocean roar.

Misty Beginnings

Morning mist with a sneaky grin,
Hides beachcombers looking for fin.
A turtle yawns, it's time to play,
While parrots squabble in a fray.

In the brush, laughter starts to bloom,
Monkeys cause a ruckus, we assume.
A peacock prances, feathers wide,
Strutting proudly, with flamboyant pride.

Awakening Wildlife

Kookaburras call with fervent cheer,
As iguanas wiggle closer here.
A gopher makes a grand debut,
While old mangroves shake it too.

The playful breeze dances through the trees,
Chasing off the night's unease.
Crickets hush, it's morning's jive,
As nature stirs, come alive!

Ocean's Gentle Hues

The sea winks at the sun,
A fish dances in its hat.
It's wearing shades of blue,
Now, who's the real acrobat?

Seagulls squawk a silly tune,
While crabs attempt a jig.
One slips and does a twirl,
Cheering crowds, oh what a gig!

Shells collect a morning laugh,
As waves tickle the shore.
A dolphin flips with glee,
And splashes us some more!

The tide brings in some jokes,
Like seaweed wearing pants.
With every wave that rolls,
Comes laughter, sea and dance!

The Dawn of Paradise

A rooster crows in shades of pink,
While monkeys trade their hats.
Palm trees sway with gossip, too,
As laughter spills from mats.

The sun peeks from behind the hills,
To see what fun's in store.
And here comes Mr. Tortoise,
Who forgot his home once more!

Banana boats begin to race,
And crabs join in the fun.
'Catch me if you can!' they say,
As they dash beneath the sun.

Cocktails made of gooey fruit,
Are sipped upon the sand.
With giggles, smiles, and silly straws,
Joy spreads throughout the land!

Warm Breaths of Morning

In the morning glow, we wake,
To find a bird on toast.
It chirps a tune so cheeky sweet,
Who knew it loved the roast?

A breeze whispers through the leaves,
And tickles at our toes.
The iguana joins the band,
And dances in a pose.

Mango juice spills everywhere,
As laughter fills the air.
We try to catch it with our cups,
But it's a fruity dare!

The sunshine wraps us in its arms,
While coconuts agree.
Let's have a party, wild and bright,
And dance with glee by sea!

Colorful Array Above

The sky's a canvas, splashed with glee,
With clouds that look like cheese.
A parrot jokes, "What's on your mind?"
"Oh, just a slice of breeze!"

Rainbow kites fly high and proud,
As kids run with delight.
One kite dives and lands on me,
It's now a colorful sight!

Pineapples wear glittery crowns,
As coconuts giggle too.
They chat about the party plans,
And how to serve the stew.

With laughter spilling everywhere,
The sun shines bright and bold.
Join us in this playful dance,
Where joy, in waves, unfolds!

Early Sunshine Serenade

The sun peeks up, a little yawn,
Birds are chirping, singing on and on.
A coconut falls, bumping my head,
Guess that means it's time for bread!

Flip-flops flop, what a silly sound,
Running to catch the dog who's found,
A puddle to splash in, oh what a mess,
Looks like fun, I must confess!

Lizards dance on a fence nearby,
With their fancy moves, oh my, oh my!
While my coffee's getting cold,
I start to grin, feeling bold!

So here's to laughter, sunshine, glee,
In this crazy morning jubilee.
Let's dance with shadows, swim with rays,
Embracing joy in funny ways!

Cacao Dreams at Daybreak

Chocolate clouds float in the breeze,
Mice sipping cocoa under the trees.
A squirrel shows off a nutty ballet,
While I spill my drink just to say hooray!

The aroma's rich, tempting and sweet,
I trip over my own two feet.
The rooster crows with a chocolate twist,
Gobbling dreams on a breakfast list!

Butterflies laugh, they zip and zoom,
Getting caught in my breakfast's plume.
Bananas breakdance, who knew they could?
In this magical world, everything's good!

So here's to mornings with a whimsie touch,
Where every pastry is loved so much.
A sprinkle of joy, a dash of cheer,
Cacao dreams make the day sincere!

Morning's Fickle Kiss

The sun smirks wide, then hides away,
Like a kid playing peek in the day.
My hair's a tangle, wild and free,
Compliments from my mirror? Not likely!

Coffee spills, a brown sea on the floor,
The cat gives me judgment, oh let's explore.
Shadows stretch with a lazy hug,
While my slippers wiggle snug as a bug!

Grasshoppers bounce, doing their best,
While I chase them in a morning quest.
Each step a stumble, a tiny mischief,
Yet laughter blooms, stirring up the sniff!

So embrace the fickle, the giggles, the flops,
In this sunny realm where the fun never stops.
With every new moment, a silly twist,
Goodbye to trouble, oh how I insist!

Crystalline Reflections Above

The sky wears diamonds, a dazzling dress,
While waves clap hands, causing a mess.
A crab in shades tries to strut his stuff,
But slips on a shell, that's quite enough!

Pineapples tumble, laughter their song,
As I giggle at fruits that just don't belong.
The fish wave bye with shiny scales,
Whispering secrets of silly tales!

Raindrops shimmer, a dance on the ground,
A cat in a puddle, oh how profound!
Bubbles burst in joyful surprise,
As a parrot winked, oh how he flies!

So here's to the sparkles, the quirks of the morn,
In this glimmering magic where joy is reborn.
With every reflection, a wink and a sway,
Let's treasure the moments in a fun, silly way!

Nature's Morning Lullaby

The sun peeks out with a wink,
As the roosters dance and clink.
Coconuts roll like bowling balls,
While the lazy iguana sprawls.

Parrots squawk a morning tune,
Sipping nectar, under a moon.
The crabs now wear tiny hats,
Wobbling past, snickering at cats.

The scent of flowers fills the air,
Bees wearing shades, with utmost flair.
Monkeys swing with giggles bright,
Chasing shadows, a comical sight.

And as the clouds drift overhead,
The hammock sways, they snooze instead.
With a yawn, they wake in shock,
Stumbling on the sandy rock.

Awakening Flora and Fauna

The flowers stretch their petals wide,
As tiny ants begin to slide.
A pineapple's grin, quite absurd,
Shakes its fronds, chirps unheard.

Lizards play tag on the fence,
Wearing shades, with no pretense.
Palm trees sway with rhythmic grace,
While sloths win races, at a slow pace.

The sun's bright rays tickle the leaves,
Where laughing frogs twirl and weave.
A mango sneezes, drops to the floor,
And giggles roll from one to four.

Insects jam out to their beat,
Making dance floors with tiny feet.
As night bows down to a cheerful day,
The fun continues in their quirky way.

Dawn's Melodic Whisper

The whispers rise with soft delight,
As crickets chirp their last goodnight.
Beneath the trees, the shadows prance,
While grasshoppers lead a crazy dance.

The suntickles turtles on the shore,
Making them chuckle, wanting more.
A hummingbird dances, oh so spry,
With shimmery moves that catch the eye.

Bananas wear pajamas with flair,
As monkey mimes jump everywhere.
Coconuts giggle, wobble with ease,
While frogs ribbit jokes, aiming to please.

The dawn is filled with laughter bright,
As nature's stage prepares for flight.
And as the day rolls into play,
Let's laugh and cheer this funny way.

Vibrant Awakening

Greenery splashes in hues of glee,
While the sun grins wide at sea.
Mosquitoes dance, seeking a bite,
While mangoes giggle at flight.

A toucan drops a fruit on a snail,
Who mutters a joke, it's never frail.
The waves laugh, splashing by the shore,
As crabs engage in a silly chore.

As orchids twirl with joyful cheer,
The laughter echoes for all to hear.
Parrots wear socks, bright and bold,
Making jokes that never get old.

Kooky creatures join in parade,
In a vibrant world where fun was made.
With each sunrise, joy's in sight,
A frolicsome feast of pure delight.

The Sun's Gentle Introduction

A big orange ball peeks from the east,
It yawned, stretched, and released a feast.
Birds tweet their morning tune,
While squirrels dance under the moon.

Palm trees shake their sleepy heads,
As the sun paints gold on sleepy beds.
A lizard does its morning jig,
Wearing a smile that's quite big.

The ocean giggles, flicks its tail,
A fish leaps up, a daring fail.
With splashes loud and whistles bright,
It's a comedy show of sheer delight.

So let's embrace the warming rays,
With flip-flops on, we spend our days.
Laughing with each playful breeze,
As nature bops along with ease.

New Day on the Coast

The roosters crow, oh what a fuss,
A squirrel prances on a bus.
Seagulls crack jokes, they flap around,
While funny crabs scuttle on the ground.

The sun rolls in, like a big orange cat,
Purring as it sprawls, imagine that!
A hermit crab tries on a shoe,
It's a fashion statement no one knew.

Waves ripple in with a silly splash,
As the beach ball makes a dash.
Kids giggle as they run around,
Chasing joys that can't be bound.

With a cocktail of laughs in the air,
No worries here, just fun to share.
As the day greets us with its charm,
We throw our cares away, so warm.

Daybreak Caress

A sleepy sun sneezes, rises slow,
Like a sleepy child still in tow.
Palm fronds flap, catching rays,
Mocking the night in crafty ways.

Bubbles float in the morning sky,
A dolphin jumps, oh my, oh my!
It wears a grin, a peppy face,
Saying, 'Let's start this fun race!'

The breeze tickles the salty air,
Laughter erupts from everywhere.
Kids on surfboards looking so bold,
Sliding on laughter, tales untold.

As the day unfolds in delight,
The world dances, feels just right.
With each giggle that we share,
Morning sunshine, joy everywhere.

Waves Brushing the Shore

Waves lapping gently, whispering tales,
While seashells giggle, sharing gales.
A crab wearing glasses waves 'hello',
As a seagull steals a donut to-go.

Flip-flops flapping with a friendly sound,
As beachgoers tumble and roll around.
The sun shoots rays like a cheeky child,
Daring us all to act a bit wild.

Kites fly high, doing funny tricks,
While octopuses perform magic flicks.
Oh, how the day begins with cheer,
As waves brush in and draw us near.

With a splash and a laugh, we greet the day,
Embracing all the fun in our play.
Nature's comedy, a show of bright,
Life's everyday joy, our hearts take flight.

Radiance on the Water's Surface

Morning breaks with a splash,
Fish leap up in a dash.
Sunlight tickles the sea,
Hey, who swam here with glee?

Crabs do a funky dance,
In their shiny shell pants.
Seagulls squawk a sweet tune,
While sunbeams prance like a cartoon.

Flip-flops flop on the sand,
As sunscreen slips from my hand.
A coconut slips with a thud,
Oops, there goes my beachy bud!

Bikinis in bright hues shine,
While beach balls bounce, looking fine.
Everyone's having a blast,
Chasing shadows from the past.

Soft Whispers of Dawn.

Bees buzz, birds start to chirp,
I trip over a sleeping burp.
Coffee's brewing with a grin,
Who knew mornings could begin?

A cat yawns, claiming the best seat,
Sunshine flows, oh what a treat.
Everyone's got silly hair,
Laughing like we just don't care.

The rooster crows, what a shock,
Yet still, I can't find my sock.
Sandy toes and playful shouts,
Happiness is what it's about!

With giggles carried by the tide,
We embrace the chaos with pride.
In a whirl of colors and fun,
The day's just begun, oh what a run!

Awakening Shores

The tide rolls in with a chuckle,
Waves crash like a playful buckle.
Sandcastles peek through the mist,
"Sandy socks, you can't resist!"

Crabs hitch rides on the surfboards,
Seagulls plot with their funny chords.
Umbrellas dance to the breeze,
As sunbathers beg, "Just one squeeze!"

Children giggle, splashing around,
Buckets tipped, joy can be found.
Someone loses their bright float,
"Not the flamingo!" they bloat.

As the sun swings high with glee,
We gather for a selfie spree.
Catch the moment, sweet and bright,
Awakening with sheer delight!

Whispering Palms

Palms swaying, gossiping low,
Secrets they share with the glow.
Coconuts roll with a laugh,
"Good luck splitting me in half!"

Laughter spills like juice from fruits,
Everyone wears funky boots.
Sunscreen battles on the skin,
"Did I miss a spot?" grins the grin.

Mermaids argue in the bay,
"Who's the fairest?" they say.
Splashing jokes and silly scheming,
In this paradise, we're dreaming.

As the day drifts into night,
Fireflies join in with delight.
With silly hats and starry eyes,
We dance beneath the coconut skies.

Daylight's Gentle Arrival

The sun peeks over hills, with a grin,
A rooster sings loud, 'Let the fun begin!'
Palm trees sway, doing a little dance,
While the sleepy beach bum is caught in a trance.

Seagulls squawk their morning delight,
Chasing each other, such a silly sight!
Coconut cups wobble under the sun,
As everyone knows, the day's just begun.

Flip-flops fly as the kids start to play,
Building sandcastles, come what may!
The ocean sparkles with laughter and cheer,
Oh, what a morning, the best time of year!

Pineapples giggle, it's a fruity affair,
As waves crash softly, they dance with flair.
The sky's a canvas, painted so bright,
With laughter and joy, it's pure delight!

Luminous Visions of Dawn

The horizon blushes; oh, what a tease,
Dancing dolphins emerge with ease!
Sunshine tickles the ocean's face,
Disco vibes fill the sandy space.

Coffee brews with a fragrant swirl,
A parrot squawks, giving the world a twirl.
Tanned folks stretch like cats on the shore,
Every wave sings, 'Who could ask for more?'

Hammocks sway gently, a lullaby's tune,
See the beach ball bounce higher than the moon!
Sandcastles rise like quirky skyscrapers,
The tide won't quit; it's our playful caper!

Smiles as bright as the morning sun,
Splashing in waves, oh, this is pure fun!
Life is a party, no reason to frown,
With each giggle, we celebrate the town!

Wisps of Light and Laughter

Sunrise spills gold, like honey on toast,
Creating a scene that we love the most.
Geckos frolic, in their silly way,
As kids zoom past, 'Outdoor games today!'

Fluffy clouds giggle, they're having a blast,
While old flip-flops moldy, sit idle, aghast.
The breeze whispers secrets, oh what fun,
Inviting all creatures out for a run!

Laughter erupts as a splash meets the shore,
Whimsical waves are always asking for more.
The sunfish grins in a shiny parade,
As the palm trees wave, in a sun-drenched charade!

Join in the revelry, let worries take flight,
In this sparkly land, everything feels right.
From dawn until dusk, we'll dance and we'll sing,
Living in joy, oh, the happiness we bring!

Awakening Garden of Eden

In the morning, fruits play hide and seek,
Bananas giggle, while their skins peek.
Coconuts wobble on their lofty crowns,
As the sun tickles the sleepy towns.

Parrots squawk with colorful cheer,
While monkeys toast the day with a beer.
Lemons wear hats of vibrant zest,
In this garden, laughter is a quest.

The flowers dance, they wave hello,
To the breeze that steals the show.
Bees buzz tunes of sweet delight,
In this Eden, all feels right.

But watch your step, the ants must grieve,
When you trip on their leaf, they won't believe.
Yet in this jokesome earthly plot,
There's plenty of joy, such a happy lot!

Serene Shores at First Light

The waves salute the waking sun,
Seagulls crack jokes, oh what fun!
Shells are gossiping on the sand,
Whispering tales, hand in hand.

Fishy friends are late for work,
They trade their fins for a witty smirk.
Dune buggies play tag with the tide,
As crabs parade, full of pride.

Morning mist plays peekaboo,
With sleepy dolphins in the blue.
Jellyfish bounce with jelly-like grace,
In this serene, whimsical space.

But beware of a clumsy flip-flop,
Might send you tumbling—oh, what a plop!
In this laughter-filled, sunny patch,
Each wave rolls in with a friendly catch.

Dawn's Promise of Bliss

The rooster cracks a corny quip,
While coffee brews with a happy drip.
Mangoes chuckle on the tree,
Who knew fruits could be so carefree?

Butterflies wear polka-dots galore,
Hovering near the fruit stand store.
While toasting with papayas, no need for toast,
In this blissful land, we love the most.

The sun pops up with a grin so wide,
As tired turtles start their slide.
Laughing waves tumble, splash and froth,
In this dawn's promise, we forget our sloth.

But hold on tight, don't let it slip,
A coconut might just take a trip!
Amidst the giggles and morning rays,
Each slice of joy, we'll share today!

A Tapestry of Light

Colors burst in the early hour,
Crayons in palms in this sunshine shower.
Lizards frolic on sun-kissed rocks,
As the dawn's laughter joyfully clocks.

Palm trees sway to a silly beat,
As turtles laugh with clumsy feet.
The canvas of life in hues so bright,
We paint our dreams in this warm light.

With every tick of the rosy sky,
Chickens gossip and make time fly.
Lemonade flows in jubilant streams,
In a world where everything beams.

So let's embrace this vibrant scene,
With giggles and grins, oh how serene!
In this tapestry, life is a kite,
Flying high with friends, oh what a sight!

A Dance of Color in the Morning Mist

The sun pops up like toast, so bright,
While roosters dance in sheer delight.
Pineapples roll in joyful spree,
As monkeys giggle up in a tree.

The clouds wear pajamas, soft and white,
While critters plot their morning bite.
Coconuts drop with a playful thud,
As lizards jive in the warm, wet mud.

Each wave takes a dip in the lively sea,
A splash of fun, a gleeful spree.
Bright flowers wink in the soft breeze,
As the world awakens with giggles and wheeze.

The day begins with a chuckle and cheer,
Nature's pranks are crystal clear.
So toast to mornings, let laughter bloom,
In this vibrant, silly room!

The Rise of a New Horizon

A sunbeam sneezes, such a loud sound,
As turtles tumble around on the ground.
Bananas slip in a comical way,
While crabs hold a dance party, hooray!

The sea is bubbling with jokes untold,
As dolphins tease, so daring, so bold.
Palm trees sway, shaking their heads,
While parrots chirp, 'Get up from your beds!'

Coconuts roll like they're in a race,
With the wind blowing softly, quickening pace.
Sunshine giggles, painting the scene,
In a land where everything's carefree and green.

As day breaks forth, let the laughter fly,
A horizon painted with joy, oh my!
Nature invites you to join in the fun,
Together we greet the rising sun!

Nature's Palette Unfurled

Brush strokes of pink and rays of gold,
As squirrels in capes begin to unfold.
With every smile from the waking sun,
Creatures parade, oh what fun!

Flowers giggle in colors so bright,
With bees in shades of a tutu delight.
Turtles wear hats made of leafy green,
As laughter echoes through the serene.

Clouds puff up, playing hide and seek,
A parrot shouts, 'You cheeky sneak!'
Each ripple of water sings with glee,
While fish splash like they're on a spree.

Here comes the day, wrapped in a cheer,
With every glance 'tis humor draws near.
So dip your brush in nature's art,
And paint your joy from the heart!

Echoes of the First Birdsong

A cheeky bird sings out a tune,
While siping nectar in the afternoon.
The wind chuckles through the leaves so high,
As the world wakes up with a big ol' sigh.

A frog in a tie leaps with flair,
While fish in tuxedos swim without care.
The sun plays peek-a-boo with the trees,
As laughter dances upon the breeze.

The echoes of morning fill the air,
With giggles and whispers, everywhere.
A world of wonder begins to unfold,
As nature shares her stories retold.

So let's raise a toast to this silly new day,
With laughter and joy, come join the play!
For in the chorus of nature's song,
We find the humor where we all belong.

Echoes of a New Day

As roosters crow with glee and pride,
A monkey swings, his breakfast fried.
Palm trees wave to the morning light,
While a parrot shouts, "What a sight!"

The sun peeks up, a glowing ball,
A lizard slips, begins to crawl.
Flip-flops flop on sandy shores,
As surfers wipe out, oh what a roar!

A fish jumps high, just to tease,
While crabs dance sideways with such ease.
A coconut falls with a comical thud,
Creating chaos, oh what a flood!

The day unfolds with giggles and cheer,
As flip-flops squeak, we all draw near.
In this burst of fun, life's a game,
With echoes of laughter, who's to blame?

Coral Sky Symphony

The sky's a canvas of pink and blue,
While seagulls squawk, doing what they do.
Frogs play tunes on lily pads,
Conductors of chaos, with no time for fads.

Sunbeams dance through leaves so green,
A squirrel leaps, trying to be seen.
Fish wiggle in coral, a vibrant sight,
While a starfish wonders, "Should I take flight?"

Each wave a note in nature's song,
Dolphins leap, they can't go wrong!
An iguana nods to the beat so bold,
In this symphony, stories unfold.

The laughter rolls like waves on sand,
All creatures come together, hand in hand.
In this orchestral morning spree,
Life's funny notes set all hearts free!

Morning Mist and Mango

The sun slips in with a cheeky grin,
While mangoes giggle, who'll take a spin?
Chickens cluck with fashion flair,
Strutting 'round without a care.

Fog lifts gently, like a sleepy head,
While a turtle yawns, still in bed.
Bananas sway in a curious dance,
As ants march by in a tiny prance.

Papayas drop with a soft thud,
While squirrels plot mischief in the mud.
A breeze whispers jokes to the palm trees,
Tickling leaves, bringing smiles with ease.

Laughter bubbles in the morning dew,
As sunbeams chase clouds with a playful cue.
In this wacky venue of taste and cheer,
Life's fruity mix makes it all crystal clear!

Dance of the Dawn Chorus

The birds awake with a comic trill,
While frogs join in, with a splash and a thrill.
Each critter sings in joyous delight,
As morning breaks with a giggly light.

A toucan flaunts his colorful beak,
While crickets chirp, their rhythm unique.
An iguana sways to the beat of the sun,
In this grand show, who will be the one?

A butterfly flutters, oh what a sight,
While a cat naps, dreaming of flight.
The rhythm of waves, a dance on the sand,
While a cheeky crab scuttles- do they understand?

Together they revel, in this funny parade,
Nature's own party, no plans were made.
With giggles and rhythms, they twist and twirl,
In this dance of dawn, let life unfurl!

Lush Awakening

In the jungle, monkeys dance,
Swinging like they own the chance.
Parrots squawk with colors bright,
While sloths snooze in morning light.

Coconuts drop from trees above,
As squirrels chase a fleeting love.
The sun peeks through, a cheeky grin,
As crabs do the conga, pulling a win.

Smiles abound in leafy halls,
While iguanas strut, bold and small.
Turtles race at a snail's pace,
Who knew slow could win the race?

In this land where laughter plays,
Every dawn is full of praise.
With a splash and a jig, we greet the day,
In this lush land, we come out to play.

Serenity of Sunrise

The roosters crow, a feathery cheer,
As sleepy heads begin to steer.
A sunbeam winks, the day is here,
With coffee cups now drawing near.

Fish flip-flop, doing their best,
While my breakfast takes its rest.
Pancakes stack like a tasty tower,
While ants march in with all their power.

A parrot shouts, 'Get off my wave!'
While dolphins play, a dance so brave.
This dawn is wild, full of cheer,
Who knew mornings could bring so near?

Waking up to this bright awe,
Nature's fun, with a touch of law.
We smile and laugh at the quirky sights,
In a world where silliness always delights.

Sands of Time at Daybreak

As the tide rolls in to play its game,
The beach is calling out my name.
Sandcastles rise like dreams each day,
While crabs tiptoe, in their own ballet.

Waves crash down with a roar so loud,
As seagulls argue, proud and loud.
Buried treasures? Just old flip-flops,
But who needs gold when laughter never stops?

Kids chase waves, a splashy affair,
While sunbathers thrive without a care.
In the distance, a kite takes flight,
Its colorful tail dances with delight.

Shells are collected, stories to tell,
Of the beach's magic, cast its spell.
As the sun rises, fun takes the stage,
With laughs echoing through every age.

Rise of the Crimson Orb

At the crack of dawn, a shiny ball,
Like a frisbee thrown at nature's call.
The world awakens, all aglow,
While roosters strut with a morning show.

The ocean giggles, tickled by rays,
As fish jump high in a watery ballet.
Icy drinks await, not far behind,
To cool off laughter and unwind.

Palm trees sway, giving their best,
As monkeys comically fail the test.
With every sunrise, giggles erupt,
In this paradise, happiness is dropped.

So gather 'round, in this merry land,
Where fun and folly go hand in hand.
The orb may rise, but fun's the star,
In a world where joy is never far.

Awakening Flora

In the garden, flowers yawning,
A sleepy bee keeps on fawning.
Petals stretch, like arms so wide,
Chasing dreams from night, they glide.

The daisies giggle, tickled by light,
As the ants prepare for morning's delight.
A butterfly stumbles, can't find its way,
Wings like a kite on a breezy day.

Tulips gossip, 'Did you hear that?
The sun's a jester, wearing a hat!'
With a splash of color, the blooms take aim,
And play peekaboo like it's all a game.

Such antics show at break of day,
In a bloom-filled ballet, they frolic and play.
Nature's laugh is a joyous tune,
As morning breaks much too soon!

Salty Breezes and Morning Wishes

Salty waves dance, full of cheer,
Whispering secrets for all to hear.
Seagulls gossip, swoop and dive,
While crabs play chase, feeling alive.

A hammock swings, tied to a tree,
Wishing only for a cup of tea.
Sips of sunshine in a coconut,
Giggling voices, 'Why not strut?'

The tide rolls in, with a playful shout,
Bubbles blowing—what's that about?
Sandy toes wiggle in warm embrace,
As the ocean tickles with gentle grace.

Morning wishes float on the breeze,
Like a child's laughter among the trees.
In this paradise, fun never ends,
Where every grain of sand's a friend!

Sunlight Through the Bamboo

Through green giants, the sun peeks fast,
While shadows dance, having a blast.
Leaves crackle laughter, bathe in gold,
As nature's pranks are performed bold.

Critters scamper, on bamboo stage,
A squirrel in shades, at this age.
A lizard slips, in a lazy dance,
While dragonflies prance in a trance.

The rays tickle fingers of waving grass,
Where small frogs practice for a class.
They croak like opera stars, oh my!
Imagining they can touch the sky.

This vibrant world comes alive,
With sounds of giggles, oh what a drive!
A bamboo tale spun with delight,
As daybreak brings joy, shining bright!

Ritual of the Rising Sun

With each dawn, the world does creak,
Like an old chair, it does speak.
Roosters call, a feathery band,
Promising mischief across the land.

The monkeys stretch, with a cheeky grin,
Launching acorns, let the fun begin!
Their playful yelps fill morning air,
As they swing from here to there.

Coffee brews with the morning kiss,
A sip of warmth, nothing amiss.
The sun rises, a giant wink,
And flowers drink up the day in a blink.

This lively show, a daily affair,
With giggles and glee, everywhere.
In this carnival of light we thrive,
Where every moment feels so alive!

Beneath the Canopy's Glow

Under leaves that sway and dance,
I saw a squirrel in a prance.
He dropped his acorn, what a sight,
It rolled away, oh what a fright!

A parrot chuckled, loud and clear,
While monkeys swung with such a cheer.
I tripped on roots, lost my shoe,
And laughter echoed, just like dew.

Cleansing Waves at Breaking Day

The waves came crashing on the shore,
They tickled toes, then asked for more.
A crab skittered, quick and sly,
I waved it off, it waved goodbye!

A seagull dove for breakfast, bold,
Snatching snacks, or so I'm told.
I tossed a chip; it flew away,
Fish laughed at me, 'Hey, that's our play!'

The Morning's Gentle Embrace

Sun came peeking through the trees,
A soft stroke like a morning breeze.
I yawned so wide, my face did stretch,
Nearby a lizard said, 'Catch!'

Tongs of sunlight on my snack,
Glow of gold, but watch your back!
A hummingbird with a funny hum,
Attempted to dance, but fell so dumb!

Coral Skies and Glistening Sands

The sky wore polka dots of pink,
While a fish danced, what a blink!
Shells were laughing on the ground,
'We're next!' they cheered with glee abound.

Footprints zigzagged in the sand,
A crab declared, 'This is my land!'
While I blushed, an octopus waved,
And asked if I had misbehaved!

Kiss of the Soft Breeze

A gentle tickle on my nose,
The wind is playing, who knows?
A dance of leaves, oh what a show,
Nature's laughter, high and low.

Birds in pajamas, singing loud,
The sun peaks out, feels so proud.
I trip on roots while holding tea,
Oops! Who knew, they were here for me?

Squirrels wear hats, and monkeys cheer,
As coffee brews, I feel no fear.
The world awakens, what a scene,
A cartoon land, fresh and green.

With every giggle in the air,
There's mischief lurking everywhere.
So let us dance, skip, and sway,
In joy and laughter, start the day!

Sunrise Reverie

In morning light, the ants parade,
Waving tiny flags, they invade.
A roach did moonwalk, quite the sight,
As morning broke, it took to flight.

With pancakes flipping on the stove,
A toast to toast we all will probe!
But syrup spills, it lands on me,
Now I'm part of breakfast, see?

Bumblebees hum a funny beat,
As frogs in ties begin to greet.
A peacock struts, proud of its plume,
With each step, it clears the room.

A glorious start, what can I say?
Let's whip up fun the silly way!
In laughter's grip, we clasp and sway,
To greet the morn, hip-hip-hooray!

Garden Awakens with Light

Sunflowers stretch, yawning wide,
Tickled by the breeze, they slide.
Daisies giggle, roll and spin,
While toads dress up in suits of skin.

The butterflies start their own race,
While bees complain about their pace.
A ladybug asks for a ride,
Following nature's silly tide.

A rusty gate sings rusty songs,
While worms sway to beat of wrongs.
With veggie hats and fruit attire,
We'll dance till our dreams catch fire.

So grab a shovel, and let's dig deep,
Plant seeds of joy, in laughter leap!
The garden blooms with every glance,
In this bright world, let's take a chance!

Radiant Colors in the Canopy

In the trees, a parrot scoffs,
A sound that seems to quite the laughs.
With colors bright, they play a game,
A feathered circus, quite the fame.

The monkey swings and starts to chat,
Telling tales of this and that.
While frogs play chess on lily pads,
The turtles sigh, they've had it bad.

A rainbow spills across the sky,
As butterflies pass by and sigh.
With every flit, they paint the air,
In this wild scene, we have a fair.

Joy bells ring in a leafy drum,
As night's retreat, the sun will come.
With smiles and glee, let's sing along,
In nature's world, we all belong!

www.ingramcontent.com/pod-product-compliance
Lightning Source LLC
Chambersburg PA
CBHW050317100526
44585CB00016BA/1528